Out For Th

or

How Would You Like Your Stake?

A vampire yarn

Martin Downing

Samuel French—London
New York-Toronto-Hollywood

OUT FOR THE COUNT
or
How Would You Like Your Stake?

First produced at Leeds University in June 1985 with
the following cast of characters:

Jonathan Farquhar	Ian Davies
Mina Sewer	Anneli Conroy
Lucy	Clare Hudson
Rennet	Simon Wilkinson
Bridget	Sharon Gilham
Dr Arthur Sewer	Richard Bacon
Constance Sewer	Rosie Sanders
Professor Hertz Van Hyer	Adrian Whyte
Count Nolyard	Martin Downing

CHARACTERS

Jonathan Farquhar, a depressed young man
Mina Sewer,* Jonathan's fiancée and Dr Sewer's daughter
Lucy, Mina's cousin
Rennet, an inmate of Dr Sewer's Asylum
Bridget, Dr Sewer's cook
Dr Arthur Sewer,* Head of Whitby Asylum for the Insane
Constance Sewer,* Dr Sewer's wife
Professor Hertz Van Hyer, of Wittenburg University
Count Nolyard, the new owner of Canthrax Abbey

*Sewer is pronounced "Seweur"

The action takes place at Dr Sewer's lunatic asylum in Whitby

Time: the present

To John Bedding, for all his kindness, understanding and support.

OUT FOR THE COUNT
or
How Would You Like Your Stake?

SCENE 1

The sitting-room of Dr Sewer's house. It is early evening and the sun is setting

It is an old-fashioned room and has the air of being much lived-in. There is a sofa C with a low table in front of it and with armchairs angled on either side. Doors L and R lead to the kitchen and dining-room respectively, while an exit UCL leads to the rest of the house. There is a window UR looking on to the grounds. UC there is a table and two chairs, and the rest of the wall space is taken up by bookcases. Against the wall UL there is a drinks cabinet. There are curtains at the windows and rugs on the floor. Above the table UC there is a large, framed portrait of Sigmund Freud. There is an ashtray on the coffee table and a single, small volume on psychology. A standard lamp is by the drinks cabinet

As the CURTAIN rises, Mina Sewer and Jonathan Farquhar are seated at the table UC. Mina is doing a jigsaw while Jonathan looks on, his face a picture of abject misery. Both are wearing old-fashioned clothes and Mina's hair is piled up. They are both in their early twenties

Jonathan (*abruptly*) Mina, do you still love me?
Mina (*surprised*) Why, Jonathan, what a thing to ask!
Jonathan It's just that you never say so any more…
Mina That's not true, darling! I distinctly remember telling you I loved you on September the sixth.

Jonathan That was two weeks ago!

Mina Was it?

Jonathan Yes, it was. And since then, not a word... Nothing that a fellow could infer affection from, at any rate...

Mina I'm sorry, Jonathan. But you know what they say—familiarity breeds contempt!

Jonathan You never kiss me, either!

Mina Yes, I do. Once a month.

Jonathan But we're engaged to be married, damn it! As your husband-to-be, I have a right to more than twelve kisses a year!

Mina Do you? I don't recall any of the etiquette books saying so. But if it worries you, I'll re-read the relevant chapters! (*She frowns*) I'm sure one of these pieces is missing... Are you certain Rennet hasn't been in here? He'll eat anything!

Jonathan (*leaping to his feet*) Oh, forget the jigsaw, Mina! Let's talk about us! (*He reaches for her hand and pulls her to her feet*) I love you, Mina. I love you more than anything in the whole wide world! (*He bends her back over his arm and kisses her*) When are we going to be married? When, Mina—when?

Mina (*still bent backwards over his arm*) Oh don't, Jonathan. You're putting me in an impossible position...!

Jonathan Why?

Mina (*struggling desperately to stand upright*) I've got cramp!

Jonathan (*releasing her*) It's true. You *don't* love me. I can tell!

Mina Oh nonsense! I've got *faultless* facial control...

Jonathan (*turning away*) If you don't love me, Mina, I'm warning you—I'll do something desperate ... something you'll regret!

Mina Such as?

Jonathan Throwing myself off a cliff!

Mina You're too impetuous, darling—and you really don't know me at all well!

Lucy hurries in from the kitchen. She is an attractive girl, slightly younger than Mina. She is in a state of high anxiety

Lucy (*breathlessly*) Oh, thank goodness I've found you, Jonathan!

Jonathan Why, what's the matter, Lucy?

Lucy It's Uncle—over in Ward X—he needs your help!
Mina (*alarmed*) Ward X! That's where the violent patients are kept!
Jonathan Has one of them escaped?
Lucy Oh, no. Uncle's just tried on one of the new straitjackets and he's stuck. He wants you to help him out of it.
Jonathan I'll see what I can do.

Jonathan exits L

Mina sits down and continues with the jigsaw

Lucy (*turning to Mina*) I'm sorry for disturbing you both, dearest Mina—really I am. But the circumstances were such that…
Mina (*drily*) You had the perfect excuse! I quite understand, dear Lucy. But you weren't disturbing anything…
Lucy Oh. (*She smiles pointedly*) I thought Jonathan looked rather distraught…
Mina We couldn't find the last piece of Miss Piggy.
Lucy (*puzzled*) Miss Piggy? (*She realizes*) Oh, I see—you're doing the Muppet jigsaw! Isn't that it *there*? On top of Kermit's *nose*?
Mina So it is.
Lucy (*pointedly*) I wondered whether Jonathan might have been worried about—well, you know—his *problem*. One doesn't like to mention these things by name…
Mina (*glancing up*) His *impotence*?
Lucy Er—yes!
Mina (*blandly*) Father's still giving him treatment for it, of course. Mainly hypnotism. But it doesn't seem to be working…
Lucy Well, *you*—I mean *Jonathan* should know … shouldn't he?
Mina So he asked Father if he should stop the treatment.
Lucy What did he tell him?
Mina To keep it up, no matter what!
Lucy Oh! (*Suddenly*) Guess who's coming to dinner?
Mina Sidney Poitier?
Lucy Oh, be serious, Mina!
Mina I have no idea. I didn't know we were entertaining.

Lucy We're not. But that's not stopping him!

Mina Him? *That* narrows the field… The vicar?

Lucy No.

Mina That *exhausts* the field! No-one else we know is that desperate for a free meal! It must be a *stranger*… Who is it?

Lucy I don't know his name—but, dearest Mina, would you believe—he's a *Count*!

Mina (*incredulously*) I *don't* believe…

Lucy It's true. He's just bought Canthrax Abbey…

Mina Whatever for? It's falling down!

Lucy Perhaps he wants to rebuild it…

Mina But it's full of rats!

Lucy So's our West wing—but *we're* sitting tight!

Mina (*suddenly*) Is he married?

Lucy I've no idea. He's only just moved in.

Mina But no strange woman's been round asking to borrow some sugar?

Lucy No.

Mina (*confidently*) Then he's probably single. (*She rises and moves toward the door*)

Lucy Mina—where are you going?

Mina To change for dinner. I want to make the best possible impression on this mysterious Count.

Lucy But you don't believe he is a Count!

Mina I'm only calling him that for convenience, until I'm sure and I intend to make *very* sure. But no matter *who* he is or *what* he plans with that rat-infested old ruin—one thing I do believe, dearest Lucy, tonight I might be meeting a man who is *neither* a *raving lunatic* nor *sexually deficient*… And I want to look my best!

Mina exits UC *in a jubilant manner*

Lucy (*staring after Mina*) Poor Jonathan!

There is a sudden commotion off L

Bridget (*off*) Git out of me kitchen, you dirty little divel! If Oi've told you once, Oi've told you *tirty times*—git out!

Rennet, a rather dirty and dishevelled young man in ill-fitting clothes suddenly bolts on stage L. He glances round quickly and then hides behind the settee

Bridget follows. She is a rather formidable middle-aged woman wielding a rolling-pin. Her sleeves are rolled up and she clearly means business

(*Loudly*) An' don't you dare hide in there, oither! (*She sees Lucy*) Oh, good evenin', Miss Lucy… Oi didn't know you were in here…

Lucy Is something the matter, Bridget?

Bridget Would Oi be makin' such a palaver if there weren't? This wee divel was tryin' to make a meal of me best slippers!

Lucy (*looking towards the sofa*) Oh no, Rennet, not again!

Bridget Yes, bejasus! But Oi caught him in the nick o' toime—tank God! Oi don't moind him eatin' the bugs—but me *best slippers*! (*She looks over the sofa*) You're a horrid little pervert that's what you are!

Rennet (*nervously*) Heh, heh!

Bridget (*to Lucy*) The day before yesterday, saints preserve us, he ate a pair of your uncle's brogues—and on Monday he almost choked himself on a wellington! Moind you, that would have put paid to his mischief for good—not a bad ting oither, when you tink of the proice of shoes! (*She shouts over the sofa*) If Oi catch you in that kitchen once more, Oi'll bate you black an' blue, so Oi will! Oi've got enough on me plate cookin' dinner for some heathen Count without chasin' you round the Baxie!

Rennet (*still hidden*) Heh, heh!

Bridget Oh, boy the way, Miss Lucy—Oi ought to tell you— there's been a stranger here askin' to see your uncle…

Lucy (*puzzled*) A stranger? What do you mean?

Bridget Someone Oi don't know! Oi tink he's a travellin' sales-man!

Lucy Why?

Bridget He troied to get me to put on a cross! He was carryin' half a dozen of them. But Oi told him Oi've already got ten of the tings upstairs! What would Oi be wantin' another for?

Lucy How strange!

Bridget Oi tought so, too! Anyway, he still insisted on seein' your uncle, so Oi told him to call round later, when the Doctor would be back from the wards. Oi hope Oi did the right ting?

Lucy Yes—yes—I'm sure you did…

Bridget Well, Oi'd better be gettin' back to the kitchen. Oidle words peel no parsnips, as me dear old mother used to say! (*She turns to the sofa*) As for you, you wee demon—moind what Oi said, or Oi'll have your guts for garters!

Bridget exits

A second or two later, Rennet creeps out from behind the sofa. He is grinning mischievously, cupping something between his hands

Rennet (*slyly*) Miss Lucy…

Lucy What?

Rennet I've got something to show you.

Lucy Oh no, Rennet! Not another cockroach!

Rennet shakes his head

A spider?

Rennet shakes his head

I hope it's not one of the cat's nasties! You know you aren't allowed to bring them into the house.

Rennet continues to shake his head

What is it then?

Rennet (*triumphantly, opening his hands to show her*) It's a Mars!

Lucy (*enviously*) A *Mars*! Oh, Rennet, where did you get it? Are there any more?

Rennet No—afraid not…

Lucy Will you let me have a bite of yours, then? I'm famished!

Rennet I might… I just might. Heh, heh! (*He unwraps the Mars bar and takes a bite*)

Lucy watches him hungrily

Do you like me, Miss Lucy?

Lucy (*startled*) What? Well, I've never thought about it…

Rennet takes an even bigger bite of the Mars

(*Quickly*) But, yes, I'd *say* I like you!

Rennet (*surveying her quizzically*) Tell me more…!

Lucy (*staring at the Mars in frustration*) You—you have nice eyes. Yes, and a nice smile!

Rennet But…

Lucy Well, it's just that some of your little habits are quite revolting!

Rennet A real turn-off, huh?

Lucy Absolutely!

Rennet (*pointedly*) Ah—but if you were a *believer*, Miss Lucy … *then* you'd understand.

Lucy (*nonplussed*) A believer?

Rennet In the *Power of Blood*! You see, Miss Lucy, Blood is the Life! Blood is Everything!

Lucy (*perplexed*) I see… Is that why you're always eating … *you* know…?

Rennet Bugs and things? Yes. (*Suddenly*) But it's not enough any more. I must have real blood now!

Lucy (*dubiously*) Well, I know there can't be much nourishment in a pair of brogues, but surely…?

Rennet (*loudly*) It has to be blood!

Lucy Rennet, that's disgusting!

Rennet It must be fresh!

Lucy Where from?

Rennet Only the Master can provide!

Lucy You mean, Uncle?

Rennet (*angrily*) No! The Master—the *Master*!

Lucy I don't follow you…

Rennet (*gleefully*) You'll follow the Master, though! Oh yes, indeed!—heh, heh! (*He moves* UC)

Lucy (*concerned*) Wait, Rennet—don't go!

Rennet (*as he exits*) Master! I'm ready, Master! *Everything's* ready!

Rennet exits UC

Lucy (*following him off*) Wait!

Lucy exits UC

(*A few seconds later, off*) Oh, you swine, Rennet, you didn't leave any Mars for *me*!

There is a moment's silence and then Dr Sewer and his wife Constance, enter L. *He is a middle-aged man of academic appearance, wearing glasses. She is a few years younger than him, and her manner is somewhat eccentric. Both are wearing evening dress in preparation for dinner*

Arthur (*as they enter*) Pinner's been giving us trouble again, Connie. He's convinced spies are watching him from behind the laburnums. I keep telling him we *don't have* any laburnums, but he won't listen. It's enough to try the patience of a saint!

Constance (*turning on the standard lamp*) Mmmm. That's better!

Arthur On top of that, I put on one of those new straitjackets this afternoon and got *hopelessly stuck*. Jonathan had to come and help me out of it. He must have thought I was a *right* lunatic!

Constance It sounds as though you've had a trying day, Arthur.

Arthur It was, rather. What have *you* been doing with yourself?
Constance I spent the last half-hour watching a marvellous television programme on group dynamics…
Arthur The Open University?
Constance No—*Emmerdale*!

Bridget enters L

Bridget Excuse me, Doctor—but there's a gentleman to see you.
Arthur At this hour? Who is it?
Bridget Oi've no oidea. But one ting's for certain—*he's not the Pope*!
Constance Did he say what he wants to see my husband for?
Bridget He didn't noither but whatever it is, it's urgent. Roight now the doorstep's full of him! Do you want to see him or not!
Constance You'd better show him in, Bridget. Whoever he is!

Bridget exits L

I've just thought, Arthur—it might be the Count! He might have called round early to introduce himself!
Arthur Whatever for? He can do that at dinner. Unless the chap was angling for a spot of lunch as well!

Bridget enters, followed by Professor Van Hyer, a tall, gaunt individual who is wearing a long overcoat, a felt hat and scarf. He is carrying a carpet-bag

Bridget Here he is, Doctor—the man himself. Now, if you'll excuse me, Oi'll be gettin' back to me preparations, or your precious Count won't be havin' his dinner this soide o' tomorrow!

Bridget exits L

Van Hyer (*urgently, in a German accent*) The *Count*? Did she say she was cooking dinner for the *Count*?

Arthur (*askance*) I beg your pardon?

Van Hyer (*controlling himself*) I'm sorry, Doktor—I am forgetting my manners. Allow me to introduce myself. I am Professor Hertz Van Hyer of Wittenburg University.

Arthur (*nonplussed*) Oh? Good evening... (*He shakes hands*) My name is Arthur Sewer... Perhaps you've heard of me?

Van Hyer merely stares

No matter! This is my wife Connie...

Van Hyer I am pleased to meet you, Madame.

Constance Thank you, Professor.

Arthur (*hesitantly*) How ... er ... how can I help you?

Van Hyer It is I who am here to help *you*, Doktor!

Constance (*vaguely*) That's very kind of you, Professor—but we already have all the servants we need...

Van Hyer Nein, nein! You misunderstand! You are in grave danger! *Everyone in this house* is in grave danger!

Constance They're not going to cut off the supply again, are they, Arthur? I thought you'd *paid* that last bill!

Arthur (*waving aside her exclamation*) What *kind* of danger, Professor?

Van Hyer The worst imaginable! The power of the Devil himself!

Constance (*terrified*) I knew it! The Health Minister's mounting an inspection!

Van Hyer Listen to me please! A stranger has bought the estate next to yours, Canthrax Abbey—am I right?

Arthur Yes, but——

Van Hyer When did he arrive?

Arthur Yesterday.

Van Hyer (*breathing a sigh of relief*) Das ist gut! There is still time... Tell me, did either of you see his luggage arrive?

Constance As a matter of fact, yes. The removal men delivered twelve big boxes. All of them wooden, with a heraldic crest on the side.

Van Hyer (*thoughtfully*) It is as I suspected! (*Aloud*) Do you have any idea what those boxes contain?

Constance No. At first I thought they were Harrod's food hampers—but what could he possibly want with *twelve*?

Van Hyer (*grimly*) They are not food hampers, Madame. Those boxes contain nothing but *earth*!

Arthur Earth? What kind of earth?

Van Hyer Earth taken from graveyards und crypts in his own country. Earth that is foul und desecrate!

Arthur You don't say! What is the chap—*a mushroom farmer*?

Van Hyer (*losing patience*) Nein, nein, *nein*! This man—this *Count* who has so quietly und secretly moved into a house within a mile of your own, is a *vampire*—a creature of the night und of Hell!

Arthur ⎱ (*together*) Oh.
Constance ⎰

Van Hyer (*with rising emotion*) He has come here with one purpose only—to prey on your household und drain its lifeblood! Tell me, are there any young women living here?

Constance Apart from *me*?

Van Hyer I said *young*, Madame! *Young!*

Constance My, you are choosy! Well, we have our niece Lucy living with us…

Van Hyer (*quickly*) How old is she?

Constance Twenty-two—and very lonely, poor pet! I was rather hoping that she and the Count might——

Van Hyer (*interrupting*) Don't even *think* of it! If you only *knew*! (*He shakes his head fiercely*)

Constance Well, if you say so. Then there's our daughter Mina, of course——

Van Hyer (*vehemently*) Ach—*two*?

Constance Bless you! But she's engaged to Jonathan Farquhar, so she's not so susceptible.

Van Hyer I would not be so sure, Madame. Do not count your chickens in one basket. (*Wearily*) Gott in Himmel, it is worse than I feared—the pickings are ripe! I must have time to think… (*To Arthur*) Dinner is served *when*?

Arthur Eight o'clock…

Van Hyer (*looking at his pocket watch*) That is in half an hour. I must hurry! I do not want the Count to see me or even know I am here…! (*He opens his carpet-bag*) Until I have worked out a plan, you must take these—(*he produces a handful of crosses on chains*)—as a precaution. Give one to each member of the household und tell them to wear it at all times. It is the only way to ensure safety… (*He closes his carpet-bag and turns to go*) Now I must leave you for a short while. But be assured, I shall not be far away. I will be watching und waiting!

Van Hyer exits L

Arthur and Constance watch him go

Constance He sounds like a maître d'…
Arthur (*putting the crosses on the coffee table*) What a peculiar chap!
Constance Do you think we should have asked him to stay to dinner?
Arthur (*shaking his head*) You know how Bridget always fusses about last-minute alterations, dearest… Besides, the chap seems to have a very poor opinion of this Count fellow. It would probably only lead to after-dinner dissension and indigestion all round!
Constance (*sighing*) Best to be on the safe side, I suppose… (*She picks up the crosses, rises and goes to put them on top of the drinks cabinet*) I do hope the Count's punctual. Bridget will only complain if we have to hold dinner back…
Arthur I should think our *main* problem's holding it *down*!
Constance (*reprovingly*) Arthur…!

Lucy and Mina enter UC *followed by Jonathan. All are wearing evening dress. Jonathan looks disconsolate, the girls radiant*

Ah! Just in time for sherry, my dears. Arthur?

Arthur goes over to the drinks cabinet and starts pouring drinks

Mina Aren't we going to wait until the Count gets here, Mother?
Constance I suppose we ought to, really—but it's nice to have a bit
of a head start when entertaining strangers… One never knows
when a risqué joke might crop up, and it's as well to relax a little
beforehand.

Arthur hands Constance a glass of sherry

Thank you, Arthur.
Lucy (*picking up the small book from the coffee table*) This looks
interesting, Uncle. Is it yours?
Arthur Yes. It's a *little*-known work of Freud—a rather startling
re-interpretation of his theory on dreams… (*He hands Lucy a
glass and then gives one to Mina*)
Lucy Really? Then it might help me to understand the one I've been
having lately… I keep dreaming about a white stallion galloping
through a field of enormous gherkins! What would Freud at-
tribute that to, do you think?
Jonathan Eating a cheese sandwich before going to bed!

Arthur offers Jonathan a glass of sherry. He takes it

Mina Oh, that's a myth isn't it, Father?
Arthur Yes. Lucy's dream would normally be attributed to a
toasted cheese sandwich!

Rennet suddenly rushes in from UC. *He is in a highly excited state
and circles the sofa, mowing and gibbering*

Rennet The Master's coming! He's here! He's here!
Constance Oh, really, Rennet—stop being so dramatic! And why
are you shambling! You're not Boris Karloff!
Rennet The Master's on his way—he'll be here any minute! (*Slyly*)
Now you'll see! Heh, heh!
Jonathan What on earth is he babbling about? How did he get in
here?

Mina (*drily*) Through the door, I imagine. Like the rest of us.
Rennet Master—they're ready for you!
Lucy Who does he mean when he says "Master"?
Constance I really don't know. At first I thought it was Paul
    Daniels, but now I'm not so sure...
Rennet (*gibbering again*) Master! Master!

*Suddenly all the Lights go out and there is a great gust of wind. The
following takes place in darkness*

Arthur Great Scott!
Jonathan What's going on?
Constance Bridget's left the back door open.
Lucy Yes—but what's wrong with the lights?
Mina Whose hand is that? (*Sharply*) Rennet!
Rennet Heh, heh!

*The Lights come back on just as suddenly as they went out to
reveal Count Nolyard standing* UC. *He is wearing full evening
dress, cloak and gloves. He is completely motionless*

The all stare at the Count. Pause

Count (*in a Transylvanian accent*) Good evening.

Pause

Arthur Er—how do you do! (*He advances to shake hands*) I'm
    Doctor Sewer...

The Count bows stiffly but does not take his hand

    Perhaps *you've* heard of me...? No?
Count (*impassively*) I am Count Nolyard.
Arthur I thought you might be. Well—ahem—may I introduce my
    wife, Connie...

Constance (*rising to greet the Count*) I'm delighted you could come tonight!

Count I, too, am delighted, Madame.

Arthur My daughter, Mina…

The Count takes Mina's hand and kisses it. Jonathan frowns

Mina (*breathlessly*) Good evening, Count.

Count Enchanté, mademoiselle!

Arthur My niece, Lucy…

Lucy (*equally breathlessly*) Hallo.

Count (*kissing Lucy's hand*) So much *beauty* under one roof!

Arthur And my daughter's fiancé, Jonathan Farquhar…

The Count and Jonathan's eyes meet fixedly

Jonathan (*coldly*) Hi.

Count (*bowing stiffly*) Hi.

Rennet (*leaping forward suddenly*) Master! Master! (*He falls at the Count's feet and embraces his knees*) Let me be your servant! I'll be faithful—I promise!

Constance Rennet—stop canvassing, and get off the Count's feet!

Rennet (*desperately*) You *will* think about it, though—won't you, Master?

Count Perhaps. I have a need for someone who knows the area well…

Rennet That's me, Master! I'm your man!

Mina (*irritably*) Oh Rennet, for goodness sake—stop pestering him and leave us alone!

Rennet (*suddenly quiet*) Very well, Miss Mina. (*To the Count*) You only have to shout if you want me…

Arthur (*threatening*) Rennet! Out!

Rennet (*quickly*) I'm going, I'm going! (*As he reaches the exit* UC *he grins ferociously*) Heh, heh!

Rennet exits

Constance I apologize for his behaviour, Count—but you must excuse him, he's not responsible for his actions…

Count He is mentally subnormal?

Jonathan (*knocking back his sherry*) No. Just a loony!

Count He seems harmless enough.

Constance Oh, he is. He just has this irrational desire to eat insects and people's footwear, and of course that's quite ruined all his social possibilities—as you can imagine. Now, before we go in to dinner, Count, would you like a glass of sherry?

Count No, thank you, Madame. I never drink wine-based beverages.

Constance How about a Bloody Mary, then?

Count Sounds terrific! Have you a *tall glass*?

Constance Certainly. Arthur?

Arthur returns to the drinks cabinet whilst Mina and Lucy watch the Count avidly

Mina Whereabouts in Europe do you come from, Count?

Count (*turning to her*) Transylvania.

Constance Is that anywhere near Marbella?

Count No, Madame. It is part of Old Europe. A country of mountains and forests, castles and villages—a land where the mists roll down over the plain…

Lucy (*fascinated*) How romantic!

Jonathan (*coldly*) Not for the plain!

Arthur (*as he hands the Count his drink*) But why are you in England? Have you come for a holiday or are you just tax-dodging?

Count (*taking the glass*) Thank you. No, I have come to make my home here.

Mina How did you travel? By boat?

Count Orient Express.

Constance I'm sure that did nicely, Count. Was it a long journey?

Count Three days from Budapest to London. Another day to reach Whitby. Not bad, considering the old myth——

Jonathan That you can't cross the Continent in under a week?

Count No. That this is the age of the train.

Lucy Did you travel first class?

Count Economy.

Arthur I didn't know there *was* an economy class on the Orient Express.

Count But surely—it is the same as your British Rail?

Constance Oh—you mean the *luggage van*! I see. But weren't you rather cramped, Count?

Count Not at all. There was more room there than in any of the passenger coaches. I lay stretched out peacefully without any risk of disturbance for most of the journey.

Mina And you could keep your eye on your cases, too! It sounds the perfect arrangement.

Constance (*rising*) Well, I think we really ought to go in to dinner, now. You'll be sitting next to *me*, Count. I *had* placed you between Mina and Lucy, but Bridget's been rather casual with the fruit cup and you'll get a better portion sitting to my left…

Count You are most kind, Madame—but I am not overfond of fruit cup…

Constance Oh nonsense, Count. You're just being polite. (*She turns to the others*) Are we all ready? Good. Then let's go in…

Constance and the Count exit R, *followed by Arthur and Jonathan*

Lucy and Mina linger for a few seconds

Mina Isn't he wonderful? So restrained, so polite—*oooh*!!

Lucy (*drily*) Now do you believe he's a Count?

Mina (*quickly*) Oh yes, dearest Lucy! I believe! I *believe*! (*She hurries to the door* R)

Lucy stares at Mina in amazement

Mina exits R, *followed by Lucy as the Lights fade to Black-out*

The same. Later the same evening

As the Lights come up, the family and the Count enter from the R. They all take up positions, either seated or standing, with the Count c

Constance I'm so sorry you couldn't eat much of Bridget's meal, Count. I should have realized you might not be used to English cooking…

Arthur Neither are we, dearest.

Count It wasn't that, Madame…

Constance Was it the *steak*? It was rather resilient…

Count No, no—it is simply that if this were *my* country—I should not be eating until after midnight!

Constance Oh, I *see*! You're suffering from *jet-lag*!

Mina The Count came by train, Mother…

Constance I know—but it's the same thing, isn't it?

Mina shakes her head wearily

Bridget enters L carrying a tray with coffee cups, coffee pot and sugar. She sets them down on the table in front of the sofa

Thank you, Bridget. (*She begins to pour*) Would you like some coffee, Count?

Count No, thank you. It makes me—(*he hesitates*)—ach, what would you English say? Makes me——

Jonathan (*innocently*) Fart?

Count (*ignoring him*) Light-headed.

Bridget (*angrily*) D'you mean to tell me you're not goin' to touch anythin' whoile you're here? What's wrong with you? You're not on one of these heathen doiets, are you? Or aren't you feelin' well?

Count (*staring at her, askance*) I am not ill—no.

Bridget (*with feeling*) You look it! You're as pale as a corpse, so you are! You ought to get your teeth into *somethin'*!

Count Later, perhaps. There is no need to worry.

Arthur Don't be harsh, Bridget. The Count was explaining to us that he's not yet used to our meal times. He would normally eat much later in the evening…

Bridget Is that a fact? Well, then, Count—Oi'm sorry for bein' so extraordinarily rude to you an' Oi hope you'll allow me to make amends boy makin' you up a doggy-bag to take home with you…

Count (*suspiciously*) What is a *doggy-bag*?

Constance It's a carton of scraps and leftovers, Count. It's a common practice nowadays for people going out for a meal to take uneaten food home with them, rather than waste it…

Count And they give this food to their pets?

Constance No—their *dependents*.

Count I see. Thank you all the same, but I have no dependents— as yet.

Bridget For the love of God, man!

The Count winces

Show some Christian charity!

The Count winces

Think of all the time Oi've put in cookin' for you!

Count (*hurriedly*) Very well. If you insist——

Bridget Oi do! Oi'll set it on the kitchen table for you. Moind you pick it up before you go!

Bridget exits L

Arthur (*wryly*) I hope you're *strong*, Count. There were enough leftovers to feed an army…!

Constance Oh really, Arthur! (*To the Count*) I'm so glad you went along with her, Count. If you refused it would have put her in a terrible state. She's cooking one of her special recipes tomorrow, and if she's upset she can't concentrate…

Count What is this special recipe? Beef Stroganoff? Chicken Chasseur?

Constance *Stew!*

Count Ah!

Jonathan Remind me to eat out, tomorrow.

Lucy (*eagerly*) Please—will you tell us more about yourself, and your family? Do you have many relatives?

Count Alas—we are not many, now. I am the only son of my particular house and I have few *living* relations. My castle is in disrepair and I no longer feel the need to maintain it. (*With a touch of bitterness*) Such is the fate of great families!

Mina How sad! (*With feeling*) You poor thing!

Jonathan raises his eyebrows in disgust

Count There is no need to feel pity, my dear Mina. I have my memories, and they are all that matter to me now. Memories of moonlit nights when the breeze was softer than a lover's breath. When the castle ballroom echoed to the tunes of the Zigeuner violins—and I would dance the Czardas with a beautiful young girl not so very different from yourself!

Mina (*coyly*) You flatter me, Count… (*She looks at him with undisguised affection*)

Jonathan scowls

Count Not at all. The compliment is deserved. If I could only transport you back to that time——

Jonathan (*drily*) A bit difficult, don't you think? Unless you happen to be *Doctor Who*!

Constance We could always put on a *record*, Jonathan… How about *Mantovani Plays Gypsy*?

Count A record?

Constance Yes—if you'd like to do the Czardas!

Count No thank you, Madame. I am not in a mood to dance…
Jonathan (*pointedly*) A bit out of practice, eh?
Count (*giving him a cold stare*) Not at all, Mr Farquhar. (*Looking at Mina*) I would much rather go for a walk in the grounds. It is such a lovely night…
Lucy (*rising and going to him*) I'll go with you, if you like! I know all the best paths and there's a really nice place where you can sit and look at the moon… (*she laughs lightly*) … it's called Lovers' Nook!
Mina (*rising and pulling Lucy aside*) But *I* want to go with him, dearest Lucy!
Lucy (*whispering*) You've got Jonathan to go out with you if you want a walk! Honestly, Mina, you are *greedy*. You even pinched the cherry off my fruit cup! (*She turns to the Count with a smile*) Shall we go, Count?
Count (*puzzled by the proceedings*) Very well, Miss Lucy…

The Count rises and Lucy takes his arm

They exit

Mina (*watching them go in dismay, then covering her face*) Oh!

Mina runs off UC

Constance (*to Arthur*) I knew there'd be tears before bedtime. There's been too much excitement today!
Arthur Can't be helped, I suppose. (*He glances at his watch*) I'd better go and check the wards—make sure everyone's locked in for the night—especially the violent cases…
Constance Do you need any help tucking them in?
Arthur If you don't mind, dearest…

Arthur and Constance move towards the door

Constance You know, Arthur—something's bothering me.

Arthur Nothing serious, I hope.

Constance Not really. I've just been wondering—who was it who analysed the psyche into the animus and anima?

Arthur (*as they reach the door*) *Jung?*

Constance No, darling—I think he was *middle-aged...*!

Arthur and Constance exit

Jonathan (*scowling fiercely, then with feeling*) Damn and blast the fellow! (*He takes a cigarette case from his pocket, extracts one and lights it. Then he starts pacing up and down, smoking furiously*)

Van Hyer enters cautiously UC. *He is carrying his carpet-bag and has his overcoat over one arm*

Jonathan does not see him

Van Hyer Is something worrying you, young man?

Jonathan You're dead right something's worrying me! (*Suddenly*) Who the hell are you?

Van Hyer (*advancing*) I am Professor Van Hyer. I called to see Doktor Sewer earlier... You must be Mr Farquhar?

Jonathan That's right. (*Curiously*) Why did you want to see Doctor Sewer?

Van Hyer I came here to warn him about something. (*Pointedly*) How was dinner?

Jonathan Pretty disgusting! (*Struck by a sudden thought*) Hey, if you came here to warn him about dinner, why the hell couldn't you have warned *me* as well!

Van Hyer I didn't come to warn him about the dinner, my young friend! Tell me—you are engaged to be married to Miss Mina, are you not?

Jonathan You *could* say that—but now I'm not so sure...

Van Hyer Why is that?

Jonathan I don't think she loves me any more. She'd rather go for a walk with that Moss Bros dummy than me!

Van Hyer (*anxiously*) She didn't, I trust?

Jonathan No...

Van Hyer I am relieved to hear it!

Jonathan *Lucy* beat her to the post.

Van Hyer (*alarmed*) Gott in Himmel! You are telling me Miss *Lucy* went for a walk with the Count?

Jonathan Yes, just now...

Van Hyer But has she taken the necessary precautions?

Jonathan Oh, don't worry, Professor. Lucy's not that kind of girl— *I think...*

Van Hyer Nein—what I am trying to say is—was she wearing one of the crosses I gave to Doktor Sewer?

Jonathan (*puzzled*) What crosses?

Van Hyer You were not given them?

Jonathan (*blankly*) No.

Van Hyer (*hitting his forehead with the back of his hand*) Ach, du Liebe Gott, what kind of stupidity am I dealing with? I expressly told Doktor Sewer—(*Suddenly*) Listen to me, Mr Farquhar, und listen well... Miss Lucy is in mortal danger. Her life—her very soul is in peril!

Jonathan That's putting it a bit strong, isn't it?

Van Hyer It happens to be the truth! You know nothing about the creature she is—is taking the air with...!

Jonathan Well, I know he's a bounder, but——

Van Hyer (*passionately*) He is more than that, Mr Farquhar. He is one of the undead, ein Nosferatu—a *vampire*!

Jonathan (*open-mouthed*) You don't say!

Van Hyer Indeed I do! A creature of the night who crawls from his coffin to prey on the blood of the living und by day sleeps like a corpse!

Jonathan (*alarmed*) Good God, man—shouldn't we go and save her?

Van Hyer All in good time! First I must tell you more about the powers of the vampire. In my years of study at Wittenburg University I learned many things...

Jonathan What kind of things?

Van Hyer (*vaguely*) Oh—*things*… Interesting things.

Jonathan Such as?

Van Hyer (*even more vaguely*) Things to do with other things… Things that happened…

Jonathan (*impatiently*) But what about *vampires*, Professor?

Van Hyer Oh, yes—vampires! They have enormous powers— strengths given to them by Satan himself. A creature such as the Count has power over most kind of animals… Animals such as the wolf, the rat und the bat. All these will obey his call, und he can transform himself into any one of them at will. He can even control the *elements* should he choose…!

Jonathan He's not what you'd call a pushover, then?

Van Hyer Far from it, my young friend! However, he is not *completely* invincible——

Jonathan I'm glad to hear it! For a minute there you had me worried!

Van Hyer There are many things he fears and avoids—garlic flowers, running water, the hawthorn tree, the sign of the cross. Any of these can put him to flight or render him powerless. But only *three* things can *destroy* him—sunlight, a silver bullet or a stake through the heart!

Jonathan Well, it's night-time now—I don't happen to have any silver bullets on me, so that only leaves the stake through the heart to finish him with. Have you got a stake, Professor?

Van Hyer (*opening his carpet-bag, then ruefully*) Nein. I am fresh out of stakes!

Jonathan What the hell are we going to do, then?

Van Hyer Improvise or panic! Und whichever it is, we must do it quickly. The longer we delay, the greater the danger for Miss Lucy. Tell me, did the Count eat much at dinner?

Jonathan No—he hardly touched his plate. Not that I blame him!

Van Hyer (*nodding*) Then he will be in a mood for some refreshment! We must hurry, or much evil will befall her. I feel it in my bones!

Jonathan That *could* be rheumatism, Professor…

Van Hyer Nonsense, young man! I am fitter than a tuba! Come with me…

Jonathan and Van Hyer exit UC

Silence

Lucy and the Count enter L. *Lucy is talking volubly. The Count looks bored*

Lucy And then I did my post-grad at Warwick. Social Studies with the emphasis on the ethnic minorities. That gave me even more insight into the problems facing our inner cities…

Count (*stifling a yawn*) It must have provided great inspiration, my dear Lucy.

Lucy Oh yes, it did. I decided I *couldn't stand* living there myself and moved out to the country!

Count A very wise decision. From all you have told me—in immense detail—at exceptional length—(*he eyes her grimly*)—greater *tedium* I cannot imagine!

We hear the sound of cats fighting

Listen to the children of the night—what music they make!

Lucy (*wincing*) You think so? Well, each to his own, I suppose!

We hear the sound of a door opening

Bridget (*off*) Git out of here, you mangy little banshees! What koind of racket do you think you're makin'? An' me troyin' me damndest to watch *Brookside*, too! Rennet, git off that tabby! You'll catch fleas!

The noise of the cats ceases and the door bangs shut

Lucy (*kittenish*) I hope you enjoyed our walk, Count?

Count (*in a non-committal manner*) I did. Thank you for accompanying me, Miss Lucy.

Lucy I was delighted to. (*Ruefully*) It's a pity we couldn't have spent longer in Lovers' Nook. If only you hadn't sat on that *sprig of hawthorn*…! Does it still hurt?

Count Not any more, I am pleased to say.

Lucy I am glad. (*She notices his hands*) Oh, look you've got dirt on your hands! Would you like to wash them? We've got hot *and* cold running water upstairs…

Count (*quickly*) No thank you. My handkerchief will suffice. (*He produces it and wipes his hands clean*)

Lucy Would you like to see round the house? I'm sure you'll like it. I can show you our new *sun-ray lamp*! Have you ever seen one?

Count No, I haven't. Later—perhaps… At the moment—forgive me—I have a slight headache…

Lucy Oh, I'm sorry. Would you like an aspirin?

Count An aspirin?

Lucy Yes—to take the pain away. I'm not sure where they're kept, but I'll see if I can find one for you. I'll try not to be too long…

Lucy hurries off UC

Rennet creeps in from the R *as the Count is speaking*

Count (*drily*) There is no hurry, my dear Lucy! (*He waits until she is out of sight and then frowns, hitting the palm of his hand with his fist. He grimaces*) I do not believe it! The women at home were not at all like this… Never so forthright, so opinionated—so … incredibly *boring*! What is wrong with this girl?

Rennet (*slyly*) You know what it is, Master?

Count (*turning to Rennet*) No. What?

Rennet (*knowledgeably*) Further Education! She's had too much of it! It's spoiled her for you! Now, if it were the other one.

Count Miss Mina?

Rennet (*nodding*) Things would be different … heh, heh! She's not spoiled—oh no… She's only got one GCSE! She's *your* type, Master.

Count (*suspiciously*) Are you being sarcastic, Rennet?

Rennet (*abasing himself*) Oh no, Master, no! I'd never dream of being sar—sar—whatever it was you said! Miss Mina's a real lady—soft, warm, yielding—ignorant! And you don't get much of her to the pound, if you know what I mean!

Count Yes, Rennet, I think I do... (*To himself*) What a vulgar creature! (*Aloud*) I shall have to try my charms on Miss Mina and see what happens. But I will need your help, Rennet...

Rennet (*eagerly*) You can count on me, Count!—I mean, *Master*! I'll do anything for you—anything! (*Slyly*) But it will cost you, heh, heh!

Count (*sighing*) I knew there would be a string attached! In the old days my servants were content to grovel and cringe, expecting nothing for their services.

Rennet But this is England, Master! Haven't you heard of the cost of living?

Count I hadn't, no—but I'm learning fast! What do you want?

Rennet The same as you, Master—*blood*! *Lots of it!*

Count And how do you think I can manage that? I have endless difficulty obtaining it myself!

Rennet I'm an optimist, Master! Heh, heh!

Count But you do not understand the risks involved! Whenever I venture forth from my coffin in search of sustenance, I am in constant danger. From sunlight, hawthorn and running water! Do you *know* how much *running water* there is in the world? Rivers, seas, streams, lakes, open drains, fountains—not to mention *rain*! On wet nights I am obliged to bite my fingernails for nourishment! It is not amusing, my friend... Then there are the crosses! You have no idea of the number of crosses I have been faced with in my time! First it was the *Crusades*... After that, nuns and monks spread like Japanese tourists all over Europe! They even tried to build a convent on my estate! (*Sadly*) I used to visit the cinema in Budapest, but *The Sound of Music* put a stop to that... (*He pauses briefly*) But worse, much worse than any of this are the *vampire hunters*—spry, elderly gentlemen, fanatically dedicated to my destruction. These I fear above all else, believe me— for no matter where I go or what I do to evade them, everywhere— *everywhere*—armed with portable, ruddy stakes—are *clones of Peter Cushing*!!

Rennet (*disconsolately*) Oh. I'd no idea it was that difficult, Master!

Count It is, I tell you…

Rennet But—but, I don't really want *human* blood, Master…

Count (*puzzled*) Then, what *do* you want?

Rennet Something simpler, like—say, unlimited access to a black pudding factory!

Count I will see what I can do. But first, you must help me to win Miss Mina.

Rennet Of course, Master! A bargain's a bargain! Heh heh! What do you want me to do?

Count I would like you to send Miss Mina to me as soon as you can, and then create a diversion which will occupy the rest of the household for as long as possible. Do you understand?

Rennet Yes, Master! I'll do my best.

Count Then go and find Miss Mina for me. And Rennet, remember *subtlety* is everything!

Rennet Yes, *sir*! You can rely on *me*!

    Rennet exits

    (*Off*) Oh, *Miss Mina*!!!

The Count shakes his head in disbelief and turns C, *lost in his own thoughts*

    Mina enters UC. *She stops when she sees the Count, then advances eagerly*

Mina Count?

Count (*startled*) Miss Mina! (*Aside*) That was quick work!

Mina I heard someone call my name, so I—(*She hesitates*) Did you enjoy your walk in the grounds?

Count To be honest—not particularly…

Mina (*pleased*) I'm glad to hear it!

Count I would much rather have gone with you. (*He stares into her eyes*) You are very beautiful, Miss Mina!

Mina Oh, Count—you're making me blush! (*Quickly*) Don't stop—I like it!

Count For the first time in many long years, I find my heart is affected, and the feelings I am experiencing defy expression…

Mina I'm sure you can manage it! Go on—*try*!

Count Very well… (*He reflects*) I get no kick from champagne… Mere alcohol doesn't thrill me at all—so tell me, why should it be true—that I get a kick out of *you*?

Mina Perhaps because I like *Cole Porter*, too!

Count No—it is something more profound. It is because you have *warmth*, vitality, strength! All of which make you unique among your kind…

Mina (*coyly*) I bet you say that to all the girls!

Count True—I do! But never before have I come across someone so positively gifted as you, Miss Mina… So infinitely suited to be my *bride*!

Mina Do I dare to hope—do I dare to *dream*… Are you proposing to me, Count?

Count You could call it that, my dear…

Mina Well, shouldn't you get down on one knee? It *is* usual…

Count If you wish. (*He does so*) There. Now—will you consent to be my bride?

Mina If you answer one question in return, Count…

Count Yes?

Mina (*eagerly*) Are you good in bed?

Count (*nonchalantly*) Have you any reason to doubt it?

Mina No—none at all!

Count Then take it for a fact—*nobody has ever lived to complain*!

Mina (*ecstatically*) That's what I wanted to hear!

The Count rises. Mina embraces him

Oh, Count! I'm *yours*!

Count I feel I must tell you, my dear Mina, that by choosing to live with me you will live *forever*! Your beauty will remain as it is now—constant, never fading despite the passage of the years…

Mina (*delightedly*) You mean I'll be just like Joan Collins? How
   fabulous!

Count More than that. You will join the legion of the night and
   sample delights you never dreamed existed!

Mina (*puzzled*) But I thought the Legion was for *men only*?

Count The night belongs to everyone, Mina. Especially you and I.
   I will be your king and you—you will be my queen for centuries
   to come! (*He embraces her closely*) And now, my dear, I want to
   seal our union, if you will permit me…

Mina (*doubtfully*) Couldn't we wait until everyone goes to bed?
   Someone might see us…

Count Do not worry—I am only going to … *kiss* you.

Mina (*relieved*) Oh! Yes, of course.

*The Count reaches to touch her neck and pulls down the collar of
her dress. Mina stands enraptured, her eyes closed, waiting. The
Count lowers his face to her neck and then suddenly starts, seeing
some thing there*

Count (*pulling away*) What is that—on your neck?

Mina (*unperturbed*) It's a birthmark.

Count (*in disbelief*) Shaped like a *cross*?

Mina Yes, I suppose it is…

Count (*frustrated and angry*) Ach!

Mina (*anxiously*) What's wrong?

Count Nothing! Nothing at all!

   Jonathan rushes on from L

The Count and Mina turn to face him

Jonathan (*shouting*) Leave her alone—do you hear!

Count (*innocently*) But I am not touching her!

Jonathan (*angrily*) That's not the point! I know all about *you*,
   Count!

Mina (*impatiently*) Jonathan! Haven't you any respect for people's
   privacy?

Jonathan Not when one of the people is someone like *him*!
Mina (*angrily*) Oh, for heaven's sake, Jonathan…

The Count winces

…stop being so theatrical and leave us alone!
Jonathan No. I want *you* to leave us—and I mean that!
Mina (*defiantly*) And what if I won't?
Jonathan I'll still beat him up, anyway!
Mina (*hesitating for a second, then tearfully*) Oh, really, Jonathan! *You are a party-pooper!*

Mina runs off UC

The Count regards Jonathan with wry amusement. Jonathan glares at him

Count So—you are prepared to *fight me* for the favours of your fiancée, Mr Farquhar?
Jonathan You bet!
Count Even though she has just agreed to be my bride?
Jonathan But you're *dead*! How can she marry a corpse?
Count She has an open mind. I should not worry…
Jonathan (*angrily*) But what have *you* got that I haven't?
Count (*easily*) A castle…
Jonathan *That's* falling down!
Count Real estate…
Jonathan In what? *Graveyards?* What else?
Count Better dress sense!
Jonathan Ha!
Count (*evenly*) But most importantly—her *love*…
Jonathan (*suddenly quiet*) Oh.
Count She does love me, Mr Farquhar. That you may be sure of… (*He grins*) So you see—I have more than *two good points* in my favour!
Jonathan (*with feeling*) You sod! I won't let you get away with this! Put your fists up! (*He advances threateningly on the Count*)

Count (*icily*) Be very careful, Mr Farquhar. I admire your cour-
age—but I must warn you—I have more strength in my *little
finger* than you have in your whole body!

Jonathan (*furiously*) You can't scare me, Count! *En garde*, you
bloody dago! Your nemesia is nigh!

Count (*drily*) Don't you mean *nemesis*, young man?

Jonathan Quit stalling! Suck on this, buster!

*Jonathan aims a blow at the Count who deftly avoids it, seizes his
arm and before Jonathan can defend himself, knees him in the groin.
Jonathan doubles up on the floor*

Count (*sadly*) I warned you about my strength…

Jonathan (*gasping*) But you said it was in your *little finger*!

Count I was being modest…

Jonathan You bastard!

Count (*advancing on him*) And now, my young hero, I feel it is my
sympathetic duty as victor to put you out of your misery…

Jonathan (*staring up at him*) You're not going to—to—?

Count Kill you? But of course! I have enough pursuers without
adding a jealous lover to the list!

*The Count reaches down and in one move sweeps Jonathan to his
feet, holding him in a vice-like grip. Jonathan's eyes widen as the
Count bares his teeth in a snarl*

Jonathan No!

As he shouts, Van Hyer runs in from UC

Van Hyer (*loudly*) Let him go, Count! I command you in God's
name!

*The Count turns at the sound of Van Hyer's voice and then releases
Jonathan who slumps to the floor, still clutching himself. The Count
moves away slightly as Van Hyer advances cautiously*

Count (*hissing*) Van Hyer!

Van Hyer That is correct, Count Nolyard!

Count So—we meet again…

Van Hyer (*grimly*) Und none too soon! (*To Jonathan*) Are you all right, my young friend? You are not injured?

Jonathan (*groaning*) I'm *dying*!

Van Hyer He kneed you in the nuts, ja? You have my sympathy. (*To the Count*) You *fiend*—you *devil incarnate*! Is there no end to your evil?

Count (*innocently*) But *he commenced it*! I am not to blame!

Van Hyer That is not what I am talking about. It is your *menacing* of the young ladies of the household! But I shall make sure you do not harm them—*Du Borscht*!

Jonathan (*painfully*) Oh come on, fellows—no *in-jokes*, please!

Count (*icily*) It was not a *joke*! He called me a—*a foreign soup*! Be careful you do not make me angry, Professor… You will not live long if you do!

Van Hyer It is you who haven't long to live, Count Nolyard! But perhaps I ought to call you by your *real* name, now I am certain who you are…

Jonathan (*puzzled*) His *real* name?

Van Hyer Ja! Nolyard is his real name *reversed*! Spelt properly it is—*Draylon*!

Jonathan Huh?

Van Hyer (*scratching his head*) An unusual *fabrication*, I must admit. I had rather hoped it would be *Dracula*!

Count We all make mistakes, Professor! You more than most! Your assumption regarding my name——

Jonathan (*puzzled*) Count *Draylon*?

Count Just won't wash, I am afraid!

Van Hyer Dry clean only, I understand. (*Suddenly*) But we are straying from the point! Your reign of terror is about to end, Count! For centuries you have satisfied your unnatural lust for blood without hindrance, und your victims have been countless…

Count (*yawning*) Really, Professor. You are being tedious! If you must make a speech, try to do so *without* threats or clichés, please…!

Van Hyer But now your days are numbered…

Count That is a cliché, Professor.

Van Hyer For with the help of God. I am going to put an end to your evil!

Count That is a threat *and* a cliché! I can't waste any more time listening to you, Professor. The night is short and I have much to do. (*He addresses them both*) If you dare prevent me, I shall crush you both—*like flies*!

The Count moves to pass Van Hyer, but the Professor suddenly produces a cross from his pocket. The Count hisses and raises his arms to ward if off

Van Hyer You are not going anywhere, Count!

Count (*deadly*) You think you are being clever, Professor. But there is more to my power than you realize… You can never defeat me!

Van Hyer (*smiling grimly*) Want to bet? (*With his free hand he reaches into his pocket and pulls out a gun*)

Count (*laughing harshly*) You imagine *that* will destroy me? Bullets cannot harm me!

Van Hyer Ordinary bullets, nein… But these are *silver*!

Count (*his face changing*) Streuth!

Jonathan (*grinning*) Good work, Professor!

Count (*furiously*) For this I will see you rot in hell, Van Hyer!

The Count suddenly lashes out and knocks the gun from Van Hyer's hand. As the Professor runs to pick it up, the Count raises both his arms

Jonathan Look out—he's going to turn into a *bat*!

Count What? With that bloody-hungry lunatic Rennet outside? No fear! I am going to do something much safer—*this*!

Black-out

Sounds of confused movements in the Black-out

   The Count exits

Jonathan What the——? Professor, he's getting away! Where are
   you?
Van Hyer Over here! Hurry, we must catch him before … ach, du
   Liebe Gott!
Jonathan What's the matter?
Van Hyer (*pained*) I have just banged my knee on the sofa!
Count (*off*) Tough titty, Professor!

The Lights come up

Van Hyer (*rubbing his knee*) We should have been prepared for
   this… He is no nincompoop!
Jonathan (*urgently*) We can't let him *escape*…
Van Hyer Nein! But now he is outside he will be almost impossible
   to find. (*Shaking his head*) What a pretty teapot of fish!

Sound of a wolf howling. The two men stare at each other

Jonathan (*nervously*) Is that——?
Van Hyer (*nodding grimly*) Uh-huh!
Jonathan (*looking towards the window, awed*) Flip!

   Arthur enters L, *looking perplexed*

Arthur Jonathan—have you seen any big dogs round here lately?
Jonathan (*faintly*) Big dogs…?
Arthur (*nodding*) Something very like one just ran past me on the
   west lawn. It was huge! (*He frowns*) Damned if I know what breed
   it was.
Van Hyer (*emphatically*) It was a *wolf*, Doktor.
Arthur (*relieved*) Really? Oh, good! I hate mysteries.

   There is a scream off L *and then Constance hurries in, scared*

(*With concern*) What's the matter?

Constance (*breathlessly*) Oh, Arthur—there's something *horrible* out there! In the gardenia patch.

Arthur (*shaking his head*) We really *must* make sure the patients are toilet trained. I've said it before!

Constance It isn't a *pooh-pooh*, Arthur. It's something *human*!

Jonathan ⎱
Van Hyer ⎰ (*together*) The Count?

Constance No—it's horrible, hairy and it gibbered at me as I passed! I was terrified! I thought it was Jeremy Beadle!

Jonathan (*grimly*) I'll go and see what it is.

Arthur Be careful, Jonathan. If Beadle *is* about—(*he grimaces*)—he may attempt a joke!

Jonathan (*as he goes*) I'll be careful.

Jonathan exits L

Constance (*glancing round*) Has the Count left, then?

Van Hyer Yes, Madame.

Constance Without saying goodbye?

Van Hyer I am afraid so.

Constance (*concerned*) Oh dear! I hope nothing's upset him.

She and Arthur stare at Van Hyer quizzically. He reacts uneasily, then suddenly points to the window

Van Hyer The drapes... He didn't like the *drapes*.

Constance and Arthur stare at the curtains in bemusement

Jonathan enters L, *dragging Rennet with him. Rennet is wearing a shaggy wig*

Jonathan Here's the culprit!

Everyone Rennet!

Rennet (*guiltily*) Heh, heh!

Arthur Why are you wearing that wig?

Rennet (*nervously*) I was told to—by the Master! He asked me to cause a stir and keep you busy while *he* had a crack at Miss Mina.

Jonathan (*alarmed*) Mina! Good God—he could be with her now!

Jonathan races out L

(*Off*) *Mina!*

Van Hyer (*to Rennet, sharply*) When did he ask you to do this?

Rennet (*embarrassed*) About half an hour ago.

Van Hyer (*incredulous*) *Half an hour?* Yet only now do you do your scary stuff——?! What kept you?

Rennet (*hesitantly*) Well, there were these moths, see, and some daddy-long-legs—heh, heh——

Arthur
Constance } (*together, disgusted*) Oh, Rennet!

Rennet (*calling off*) I'm sorry, Master—really I am! But I was *hungry*!

Van Hyer (*to himself, frowning*) So is *he*.

Van Hyer then looks astonished as Lucy and Mina enter UC, *the one furious, the other smiling. They are oblivious to anyone else*

Lucy (*drily*) So you were *alone* with him, were you?

Mina (*easily*) For all of *fifteen minutes*, dearest Lucy.

Lucy He must have thought it a prison sentence!

Mina (*ignoring her*) And you know—he actually *proposed* to me.

Lucy I don't believe you!

Mina It's the truth! What's more, dearest Lucy, I *accepted*.

Lucy But you're already engaged to Jonathan! Honestly, Mina, you are *two-faced*!

Mina Psychological insults won't get you anywhere.

Lucy (*furious*) Oh, won't they? Listen to me, you deceitful little cow——

Jonathan suddenly rushes in, anxious and out of breath

Jonathan Quick! We've got to raise a search-party! Find the Count
and get her back… Before it's too late!

Arthur Get who back?

Van Hyer Miss Mina's here with us…

Jonathan (*grimly*) Yes, but *Bridget* isn't!

Lucy (*wide-eyed*) *Bridget?*

Van Hyer (*urgently*) You mean the Count has——

Jonathan Come back, crashed through a window and carried
her off!

Mina (*dismayed*) No!

During the following, Bridget stomps in, looking dishevelled

Constance *That* must have been a nice surprise. She doesn't have
much fun in that kitchen, poor soul.

Bridget (*crossly*) An' Oi'm havin' no fun *now*! Oi'm bruised, Oi'm
damp—(*she grimaces*)—an' me unmentionables are all twisted!
(*She tugs at her clothing, scowling*)

Van Hyer What happened?

Bridget Oi was in me parlour watchin' TV when in flies the Count
as if he owns the place! Then, before Oi could bless meself, he
picks me up, carries me out the door an' starts spoutin' all sorts
o' romantic rubbish—tings loike me bein' his *queen of the noight*
an' other piffle!

Mina (*dismally*) Oh!

Bridget You never heard the loike of it! (*She shivers*) An' then his
lips came closer an' closer until his breath was all warm on me
neck!

Constance How delicious!

Bridget Well Oi wouldn't say *that*—but it beats scrubbin' spuds!

Lucy (*enviously*) Did he—*kiss* you?

Bridget (*crossly*) He did not! He dropped me loike a hot scone
roight boy the hoydrangeas an' took off loike a hare!

Van Hyer (*curious*) Were you wearing a cross?

Bridget (*shaking her head*) Oi'd say it was them snails Oi cooked
for supper. They leave a powerful smell of garlic on the breath!

Jonathan (*laughing*) Well, of all the…!

Van Hyer You should be grateful for your plate of *escargots*,
Bridget. They have undoubtedly saved your life.

Bridget It wasn't me loife Oi was worried about, Professor! (*She
sighs ruefully*) That Count, though—he's a foine figure of a
man…

Mina⎫
Lucy⎭ (*together*) Oh yes, indeed!

Bridget (*musing*) It'll be a shame to see him go.

Mina⎫
Lucy⎭ (*together, dismally*) *Go?*

Bridget Yes. First ting tomorrow noight, is what he shouted… Says
he's goin' home—(*clearly puzzled*)—to rest up.

Jonathan (*delighted*) Yes!

*He and Van Hyer shake hands in celebration. Mina and Lucy still
look miserable*

Bridget (*rousing herself*) Anyway—he sends his love to all, and a
special message to *you*, Professor…

Van Hyer Und what might that be?

Bridget He's sure to see you again…

Van Hyer smiles wryly

And when he *does*, he hopes you'll still be game for a laugh!

Van Hyer Well—*I* hope so, too.

Bridget Oh—an' one last ting… *Rennet's* to have the doggy-bag
Oi made up. Not that you deserve it, you little divel!

Rennet (*panic-stricken*) But I don't! I wasn't *that* bad!

Bridget (*obliviously*) Well, Oi tink that's everythin'. Now—before
you all head off to bed—do any of you fancy a *quick boite*?

Everyone (*shocked*) *Bridget!*

*Bridget stares at them in bewilderment as the Lights fade to Black-
out. As the stage darkens, a wolf howl is heard*

CURTAIN

FURNITURE AND PROPERTY LIST

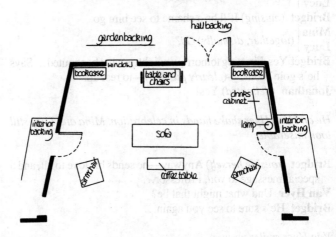

SCENE 1

On stage: Sofa

2 armchairs

Low coffee table. *On it:* ashtray, volume on psychology

Table. *On it:* jigsaw

2 chairs

2 bookcases

Drinks cabinet. *In it:* glasses, bottle of sherry, tomato juice

Rugs

Large, framed portrait of Sigmund Freud

Standard lamp

Personal: **Bridget**: rolling-pin
Rennet: Mars bar
Dr Sewer: spectacles, watch (worn throughout)
Professor Van Hyer: carpet-bag containing several crosses
on chains

Scene 2

On stage: As before

Off stage: Tray. *On it:* coffee pot, cups, milk, sugar (**Bridget**)
Shaggy wig (**Rennet**)

Personal: **Professor Van Hyer**: carpet-bag, overcoat with one cross
in one pocket and a gun in the other
Jonathan: cigarette case, lighter
Count Nolyard: handkerchief

LIGHTING PLOT

Practical fittings required: standard lamp
Interior. The same scene throughout

SCENE 1

To open:	Early evening general lighting	
Cue 1	**Constance** turns on the standard lamp *Snap on practical and covering spot*	(Page 8)
Cue 2	**Rennet**: "Master! Master!" *Black-out*	(Page 14)
Cue 3	**Rennet**: "Heh, heh!" *Lights up*	(Page 14)
Cue 4	**Mina** and **Lucy** exit R *Fade lights to black-out*	(Page 17)

SCENE 2

To open:	Darkness	
Cue 5	As the **family** and **Count** enter R *Lights up*	(Page 18)

EFFECTS PLOT

Cue 1	**Rennet**: "Master! Master!" *Sound of a great gust of wind*	(Page 14)
Cue 2	**Count**: "—greater *tedium* I cannot imagine!" *Sounds of cats fighting*	(Page 25)
Cue 3	**Lucy**: " … to his own, I suppose." *Door opens off stage*	Page 25)
Cue 4	**Bridget**: "You'll catch fleas!" *Cat noises cease. Door slams shut*	(Page 25)
Cue 5	**Van Hyer**: "…teapot of fish!" *Wolf howls*	(Page 35)
Cue 6	As Lights fade to Black-out at end of Scene 2 *Wolf howls*	(Page 39)